What If the Polar Ice Caps Melted?

Katherine Friedman

HIGH
interest
books

Children's Press®
A Division of Scholastic Inc.
New York / Toronto / London / Auckland / Sydney
Mexico City / New Delhi / Hong Kong
Danbury, Connecticut

Book Design: Michelle Innes
Contributing Editor: Matthew Pitt
Photo Credits: Cover © Carr Clifton; pp. 4, 6, 7, 12–13, 19 (bottom), 20–21, 23, 26, 28, 41 © Photodisc; p. 5 © C.M. Leask; Eye/CORBIS; pp. 9, 40 © AP/Wide World Photos; p. 10 © Chinch Gryniewicz/CORBIS; p. 14 © CORBIS; p. 16 © Caroline Penn/ CORBIS; p. 19 (top) © Dan Guravich/CORBIS; p. 24 © Robert Pickett/CORBIS; p. 27 © LLEWELLYN/Pictor; p. 31 © Richard Cummins/CORBIS; p. 32 © Roger Ressmeyer/CORBIS; p. 35 © Duomo/CORBIS; p. 36 © Bill Varie/CORBIS; p. 39 © Joseph Sohm; ChromoSohm Inc./CORBIS

Library of Congress Cataloging-in-Publication Data

Friedman, Katherine.
   What if the polar ice caps melted? / Katherine Friedman.
      p. cm. -- (What if?)
   Includes index.
   Summary: Discusses the environmental effects of the melting of the polar ice caps.
   ISBN 0-516-23914-7 (lib. bdg.) -- ISBN 0-516-23477-3 (pbk.)
   1. Global warming--Environmental aspects--Juvenile literature.
[1. Global warming. 2. Climatic changes. 3. Climatology.] I. Title. II. What if? (Children's Press)

   QC981.8.G56 F76 2002
   363.738'74--dc21

                                                2001037280

CONTENTS

INTRODUCTION

What if entire cities were covered in water? What if the temperature on a normal summer day climbed to a blazing 130 degrees Fahrenheit (54 degrees Celsius)? What if most of the animals we know today became extinct, as the dinosaurs did? What if trees and plants couldn't grow? How would we find food? Would we be able to build homes?

Could global warming and the melting of the polar ice caps really cause these things to happen? Absolutely. This book will help you understand why ice caps are so important to Earth's future. It will uncover what's happening to the ice caps. And it will also reveal steps you can take to prevent the problem.

The most impressive ice caps are found in Earth's remotest corners. Yet if they were to melt, the effects would be felt by humans everywhere.

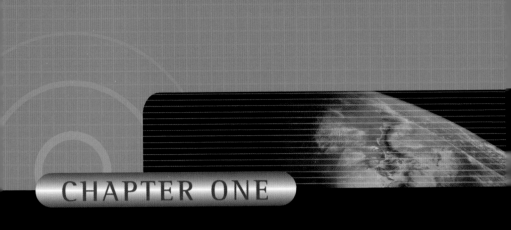

CHAPTER ONE

What Are Ice Caps?

Another name for an ice cap is a glacier. Glaciers are large masses of ice and snow. They can take several forms, such as ice sheets, ice shelves, and ice caps. An ice cap is a dome-shaped glacier. The ice caps covering Earth's North and South Poles are known as polar glaciers. The Arctic region makes up the North Pole. Antarctica covers the South Pole.

Experts believe that polar ice caps are melting because of global warming. Global warming is the unnatural rise of air temperature near Earth's surface. Scientists at places such as the National Snow and Ice Data Center (NSIDC) study satellite photos taken from space. These photos show where the ice caps are melting, how much ice is melting, and for how long

Satellites high above Earth have captured some disturbing images. They show that our planet's ice caps are melting at an unbelievably quick rate.

it stays melted. By keeping track of these things, they can tell if Earth is becoming warmer or cooler.

A global change in temperature is not very unusual. Tens of thousands of years ago, we had a period called the Ice Age. The planet was covered in snow and ice. Then the weather became warmer and the snow and ice melted. So Earth's warming and cooling patterns follow a natural cycle—usually. Today, however, Earth is heating up with shocking speed. Ice caps are melting at incredible rates. Worse, the increase in Earth's temperature shows no signs of slowing down.

Many things may cause global warming. Human beings are at the top of the list. Much of what we do—from what we buy to what kind of energy we use—causes changes in Earth's ecosystem. The ecosystem is Earth's natural environment, which includes all life on the planet.

Why Ice Is Nice

Most ice caps are in Antarctica, the fifth-largest continent. Some ice caps are about 10,500 feet (3,200 meters) thick. They have existed for more than 170,000 years. They are important for a number of reasons. They provide a home for animals, such as penguins, whales, and seals, that can survive in frigid

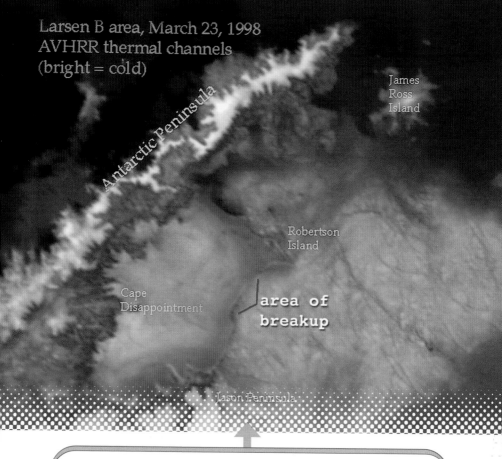

Larsen B area, March 23, 1998
AVHRR thermal channels
(bright = cold)

James Ross Island

Antarctic Peninsula

Robertson Island

Cape Disappointment

area of breakup

Jason Peninsula

This satellite photo shows where a 75-square-mile (194.3 square kilometers) chunk of ice shelf broke off in early 1998 due to global warming.

temperatures. Ice caps also act as a natural mirror of the sun's light and heat, reflecting them back into space. Without ice caps, the sun's heat remains trapped in Earth's atmosphere, adding to global warming. Changes to the ice caps affect sea levels too. If global warming causes the ice caps to melt, sea levels around the world will rise. Rising seas will cause big problems.

One of the biggest problems is that Earth's weather patterns might change. Changing weather patterns could cause places that already get enough rain to flood. Meanwhile, Earth's driest areas would go through long droughts, or water shortages. If the polar ice caps melt, life across the globe will be changed forever. The Environmental Protection Agency (EPA) reports that global warming could "raise sea levels, and change precipitation and other local climate conditions." The EPA also believes that climate changes could then "alter forests, crop yields, and water supplies. They could also threaten human health, and harm birds, fish, and many types of ecosystems."

The Earth we live in now is one we can enjoy. Though our summers may be hot and our winters cold, people can still enjoy the outdoors. People can see penguins in a zoo. They can travel to beautiful places, such as Glacier National Park in Montana. Today, you probably don't have to worry too much about having enough food and water. Can you imagine a world without all of these things? Can you imagine a world where cities are blanketed by water? It all may be happening faster than you think.

If Earth's weather patterns alter, it may mean that areas already struggling with drought could become barren wastelands.

CHAPTER TWO

Too Hot to Stop?

Greenhouse Gases

Energy from the sun heats the earth's surface. Some of this energy is bounced back into space. Greenhouse gases in the atmosphere, such as water vapor, carbon dioxide, and other gases, trap some of this energy. This keeps the earth comfortably warm. This is called the natural "greenhouse" effect. But serious problems pop up when the amount of the greenhouse gases in the atmosphere increases. Burning fossil fuels such as oil and coal for our energy needs releases huge amounts of carbon dioxide and other gases into the atmosphere. These increases make the atmosphere trap more heat than it normally would. This trapped heat causes temperatures around the world to rise. Every time you start a

Some solar radiation is reflected by the earth and the atmosphere.

Some of the radiation passes through the atmosphere, and some is absorbed and bounced in all directions by greenhouse gas molecules. The effect of this is to warm the earth's surface.

Radiation passes through the clear atmosphere.

Radiation is emitted from the earth's surface.

Most radiation is absorbed by the earth's surface and warms it.

This diagram shows the natural greenhouse effect. Radiation from the sun safely warms Earth and its atmosphere. This effect is disrupted by a build-up of greenhouse gases, which happens when fossil fuels are burned for most of our energy needs.

car, run hot water for a bath, or turn on a lamp, the blanket of greenhouse gases gets a bit thicker.

Many scientists believe that global warming may cause the ice caps to melt. In fact, each year more scientists who once thought global warming wasn't a big problem change their minds.

It may be just a matter of time before the world-famous snows of Mt. Kilimanjaro are no more.

Warmed and Dangerous

All over the world, temperatures are rising each year. You might ask, "What's so terrible about a hotter summer or a shorter winter?" The problem is that when our weather changes, even a little, Earth changes a lot.

For example, some of Earth's beauty is starting to vanish. Mt. Kilimanjaro, the tallest mountain in Africa, is covered by an ice cap. Since the start of the twentieth century, 75 percent of that ice cap has melted. Within fifteen years, it may melt completely. The glaciers in Montana's Glacier National Park are melting a little more each year. Before the end of the twenty-first century, they may disappear. If we don't halt global warming soon, some of Earth's most majestic sights could be gone for good. More important, this melting is a clear warning signal of a global increase in temperature.

Because of global warming, some people may soon be forced to evacuate, or leave, their homes. In the South Pacific there is a chain of thirty-three islands called Kiribati. People live on twenty-one of these islands.

Kiribati's islands are facing the threat of a flood that could sink thousands of homes.

Global warming causes temperatures to rise both on land and in the oceans. When the oceans warm, the sea level rises. Due to this, Kiribati's beaches are becoming flooded. If the ocean rises just 10 more feet (3 m), these islands will be covered completely by water, leaving 92,000 people without homes.

Fire and Ice

On one hand, rising sea levels could flood coastlines from New York to Miami. On the other hand, global warming could cause extreme drought in places that are already wilting from the heat. In states such as California and Nevada, the weather is already hot and dry. Fires start easily and spread quickly, laying waste to any homes and land in their path. Changing weather patterns could mean that these areas receive even less rain than usual. With no relief from the rain, fighting these huge blazes could become almost impossible.

Even today, water shortages affect many areas of the world. In California, there are times when it is illegal to wash your car or water your lawn. In 1998, thousands of people died of thirst in India because there was not enough water to drink. As summers become hotter and longer, crops in parts of Africa and India die. People from these areas die of starvation because there is not enough water to grow food.

Animal Planet

Many animals that depend on frigid conditions suffer from climate changes, too. Butterflies must fly higher and farther north each year, to avoid the heat. Fish, such as salmon, are having trouble breeding because the ocean temperature is rising. If global warming continues, many species of marine life may vanish from the seas and oceans forever.

In the Arctic region, polar bears are having fewer cubs because their mating season is being disrupted by the weather. Recently, scientists made a frightening discovery near the North Pole while on board the Russian ship *Yamal*. They were able to move through a mile-long body of water. This was in a place where the ice was supposed to be 9 feet (2.7 m) thick!

These changes may seem small. So what if there are fewer butterflies? Why does it matter if Glacier National Park is melting? You might say, "None of this will happen in our lifetime." Well, that may or may not be true. But it is certainly true that if we don't fight global warming right now, future generations will pay the price.

The South Pole isn't the only place facing problems. Polar bears in the Arctic region are threatened by global warming, too.

DID YOU KNOW?

During the Ice Age, it took a temperature increase of only 9 °F (5 °C) to change Earth from a frozen block to the livable planet we know now.

Chapter Three

Degrees of Damage

Meltdown

If polar ice caps continue their thaw, life as we know it will no longer exist. Even a small temperature increase could mean big problems. After all, the temperature of the entire earth only rose 1 degree Fahrenheit during the twentieth century. Yet temperatures in Antarctica rose at a much more alarming rate: 4.5 °F (2.5 °C) in the past fifty years!

It is difficult to predict exactly how high temperatures will climb. Recently, scientists made 235 different predictions about global warming. Some said that Earth would warm 2.5 °F (1.4 °C) in the twenty-first century. Others said it could rise 10.4 °F (5.8 °C). But these predictions were 50 percent higher than

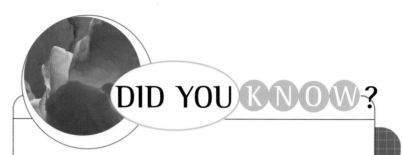

DID YOU KNOW?

The International Panel on Climate Change (IPCC) is a group of expert scientists. They estimate that sea levels will rise 20 inches (50 centimeters) by the year 2100. That amount would have a big impact on coastal cities, especially during storms.

the ones made just five years before. If we continue ignoring the problem, these predictions could get worse. The earth may be unlivable for your grandchildren. This is how their lives would be different from yours.

Change for the Worse

Antarctica is disappearing. Each year, lakes and rivers in cold climates are freezing later and thawing earlier. All this melting means that sea levels are rising. If sea levels keep rising, landmasses all over the world will flood. The coasts of states such as Florida and Louisiana will be covered by water. People would lose their homes. They would have to move farther inland to find dry land. This would lead to severe overcrowding.

Eventually, due to flooding, drought, and rising sea levels, farmers would lose their crops. In Florida's Biscayne Bay, flooding has already pushed salt water onto farmland. This salt water makes the land too toxic for growing crops. So maybe we could get food from the sea instead. But remember: Global warming has also caused a shortage of fish. Could we find enough food for dinner?

A few degrees make a difference: Floods such as this one could become common if Earth's temperature keeps climbing.

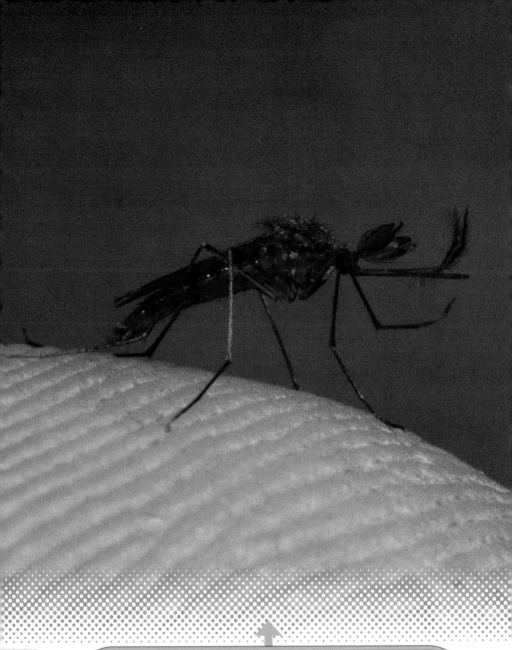

In 2001, scientists in Oregon discovered that pitcher plant mosquitoes are adapting to global warming. This eerie report suggests that warmer climates may allow pests to live longer and roam farther north.

Leaving a Bad Taste

If Earth's landmasses were covered by water, the one thing we wouldn't have to worry about is enough drinking water, right? Wrong. If sea levels rise too much, saltwater from the ocean will seep into our freshwater supply. If this happened, would we have enough fresh water to drink? We would have to find new ways to filter the salt out of the water. Though this hasn't happened yet, the threat looms before us.

Diseases could strike us as well. Insects that thrive in warm, moist weather, such as mosquitoes and ticks, carry many diseases. Some of these include Lyme disease, malaria, and Dengue fever, which causes joint pain, headaches, and rashes. Right now, mosquitoes prefer staying in warmer climates, such as the southern United States. If global warming keeps up, the army of insects will be able to move (and remain) much farther north, spreading their diseases to new areas.

The Bottom Line

Over time, even a seemingly slight change in sea level would cause disaster. There is no question that all life depends on Earth's delicate balance. Right now, that balance seems to be tipping.

DID YOU KNOW?

Experts in climate change have said that if the most dire temperature predictions come true, sea levels could rise 30 feet (9.1 m). If the temperature changes continue, the state of Florida would be completely underwater in 1,000 years!

In the United States, we have not yet felt the worst effects of changing weather patterns and sea levels. We have, however, witnessed the effects in other countries. Their plight could soon become our own. As mentioned before, our own coasts could flood. We could also find ourselves fighting unbearable temperatures and drought. But these disastrous predictions don't have to come true. There are many things that we can do to prevent the worst from showing up at our back door.

If the worst predictions come to pass, coastal towns could
be ruined by rising sea levels.

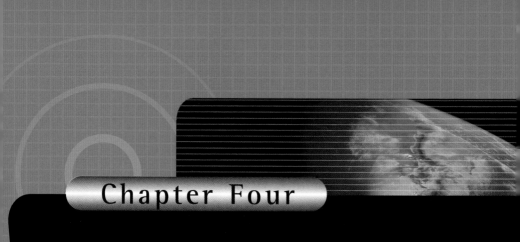

Chapter Four

Where You Come In

Can what you do really make much difference? Would it matter if you left the lights on in your room when you left for school each morning? Well, imagine millions of other people thinking the same way—leaving the shower on too long or driving to a store instead of taking a bus.

When it comes to using energy, little decisions can stack up into a big problem. When we don't think about how our actions affect Earth, it often comes back to haunt us. That is what is happening now. The energy we've wasted and pollution we've released have only added to global warming and the melting of the ice caps.

Global warming is not a distant problem. It is something that is happening every day. It is serious and scary. It is also something that we can help control. Surprisingly, the things we can do are not that difficult. Our small actions can make a big difference.

Trees, Please!

As you know, greenhouse gases are some of the worst contributors to pollution. Farms, factories, and energy plants all produce them. Yet there's a powerful weapon we can use to cut down on the carbon dioxide and methane in the air. That weapon is trees! Trees eat up carbon dioxide as they grow. Then they convert, or change, the carbon dioxide into oxygen. Finally, they release this nourishing supply of oxygen into the air. One acre of trees can soak up 5.5 tons (4.99 metric tons) of carbon dioxide each year. So go plant a tree! Even better, volunteer for a group, such as the National Tree Trust, that helps to plant trees.

New Energy Sources

The way we now produce energy contributes to pollution. Fossil fuels that run our cars, heat our homes, and power our factories poison the air with carbon dioxide. And the worst part? The United States has only 4 percent of the world's population. Yet it produces 25 percent of the world's carbon dioxide! We are the most polluting country in the world. Some people argue that we need to continue burning fossil fuels to keep our economy strong. They say that we have a lot of factories that keep people employed, so we must continue to use a lot of energy. That's true—but there are other ways of creating energy that aren't as destructive to the environment.

Blowing in the Wind

Wind power is a source of energy that does not produce carbon dioxide. At the moment, wind power is the best alternative to fossil fuels. Windmills capture the energy stored in the wind. As wind passes through the windmill's rotor blades, the blades spin and energy builds. A generator attached to the windmill then converts this energy into electricity. Right now, European nations are doing the best job of using wind power.

Solar power is another option. Solar power uses the sun's heat and transforms it into energy. Some people already use solar energy to heat their houses.

The winds of change: Some European nations are cutting back on emissions by using wind power as an electricity source.

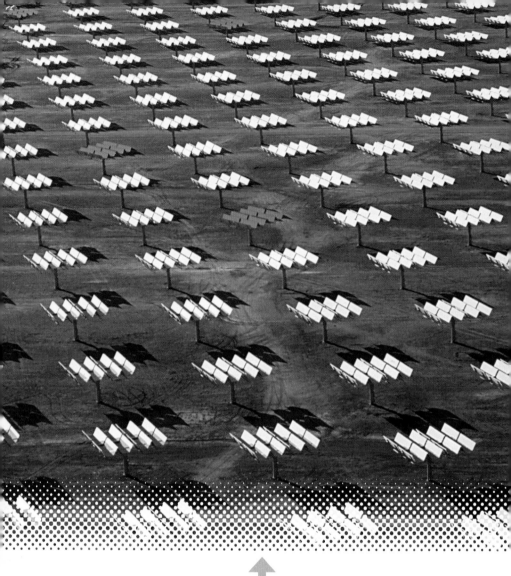

This Bakersfield, California, power plant uses 756 solar panels to catch and utilize the sun's energy.

However, many companies don't want to use solar power because of the high costs involved. Hopefully, solar power experts will soon find ways to make it less expensive.

Nuclear energy is another replacement for fossil fuels. Nuclear energy works by mixing elements together that cause a tiny combustion, or explosion. This combustion releases a burst of energy. Nuclear energy is very powerful, but can also be very dangerous. If nuclear power is carefully controlled, it can be an excellent source of energy. But if there is an accident or a leak, the results can be fatal.

New kinds of energy sources are being explored and tested all the time. One of the newest is fuel cells. Fuel cells are formed by combining oxygen and hydrogen. When they join together, they make electricity. But instead of releasing carbon dioxide into the air, they release only water. Fuel cells are being tested for use as electricity in buildings. They are also being tested as a replacement for gasoline in cars.

Small Change, Big Impact

There are small changes you can make in your everyday life that will help slow global warming. But that's not the only benefit to conserving, or saving, our natural resources. You'll be helping future generations lead healthier lives.

Pay attention to how much water you use. Don't let the water run as you brush your teeth. Try to take shorter showers each day. Don't run the dishwasher unless it's full. Keep in mind that it takes energy to heat water, so use lukewarm or cool water whenever possible. Also, when you wash your clothes use warm water instead of hot. It does just as good of a job and uses far less energy.

Use the "Goldilocks" approach to heating or cooling your home. Don't keep it too hot or too cold. Try to adjust the temperature so that it's just right.

When you travel, think about how you can conserve energy. Walk, ride a bike, strap on your in-line skates, or jump on a skateboard if possible. You can also carpool to school with friends or take public

Using bikes or skateboards to take you places will help roll
back the threat of global warming.

Remember those three *R*s—reduce, reuse, recycle. You'll be doing your part to save the polar ice caps.

transportation. If more people carpool, you'll have less traffic to fight through.

Recycle—it really works! The less waste we produce, the less energy we have to use to create new products. Reuse your grocery bags. Buy foods that don't have a lot of packaging. Not only does this help the environment, but it also saves you extra trips taking out the trash. Remember the three *R*s—reduce, reuse, recycle.

Earlier, we discussed the importance of trees and plants to our ecosystem. Keep plants in your house or on your patio. Let your parents know why you are concerned, and why you want a healthy planet. Talk to them about planting bushes and trees outside your house or apartment.

Change your light bulbs. Replace regular bulbs with "energy efficient" bulbs. These can be found at most grocery and hardware stores.

Encourage your parents to think about the earth when they shop for a new car. Most people don't need a giant truck or an S.U.V. Ask them to buy a car that gets at least 30 miles to the gallon.

Ask your parents to make your house energy efficient. Walls should be insulated so that you don't lose heat in the winter. Make sure your refrigerator, dishwasher, and washing machine are not too old. Invest in good windows so that heat doesn't escape in the winter. This also saves your parents money! Surf the EPA Web site listed at the back of this book. It provides a list of companies that use wind, solar, and nuclear power, instead of fossil fuels. Support them by using their services and products.

Write to the Top

Write or e-mail the United States Department of Agriculture (USDA). Ask them to explore new farming methods. Every time a farmer tills his soil for a new crop, it releases carbon. This carbon mixes with oxygen in the air and forms—you guessed it—carbon dioxide. If there was a way to replant crops without tilling, we could stop over 2,000 pounds (.91 metric tons) of carbon dioxide from entering the atmosphere each year!

While you're at it, write to your representatives and senators. Urge them to support laws that protect the environment. And why not even write to the president? In June 2001, President Bush's energy plan came under attack by scientists who study global warming. They discovered that his plan would make it even worse. Letters from U.S. citizens like you might make him rethink his approach to the problem. The more he hears from people like you, the more likely he will be to listen.

Our leaders make crucial choices for the environment. To make the best choices, they need to hear from people like you.

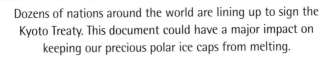

Dozens of nations around the world are lining up to sign the Kyoto Treaty. This document could have a major impact on keeping our precious polar ice caps from melting.

DID YOU KNOW?

In 1997, many nations wrote a pact called the Kyoto Treaty. It was designed to cut down on carbon dioxide emissions. In doing this, scientists believe we can help slow the melting of ice caps. In March 2001, President Bush decided that the United States should not follow the Kyoto Treaty. He believed that the costs of reducing pollution would make companies lose money. Many environmental groups were angered by his decision.

Planet Protection

By doing just a few of these things, you can help keep Earth healthy. You can help ensure that our planet will survive another millennium. For millions of years, Earth has protected us. Don't you think it's time we return the favor?

NEW WORDS

carbon dioxide a gas formed by the combination of carbon and oxygen

combustion a small explosion

conservation the process of saving, not wasting or using up, our natural resources

convert to change from one thing into another

ecosystem the environment of our planet and all living things in it

emissions gases released into the air when fossil fuels are burned

energy-efficient able to produce power without too much waste

fossil fuels natural fuels, such as coal or gas, formed from the remains of once-living organisms

fuel cells devices that can change a mixture of hydrogen and oxygen into electricity

glacier a large mass of ice moving slowly over a land area

global warming an increase in average temperatures on Earth, caused by "greenhouse gases"

greenhouse effect the trapping of solar heat in Earth's atmosphere

methane a colorless, odorless gas used for fuel

polar ice caps large bodies of ice that remain frozen all year; their existence helps balance Earth's temperature

solar power energy from the light or heat of the sun

wind power energy generated by the wind

FOR FURTHER READING

Dipper, Frances A. and Jane Parker. *Oceans & Rain Forests.* San Diego, CA: Silver Dolphin Books, 2000.

Earth Works Group. *50 Simple Things Kids Can Do to Save the Earth.* Kansas City, KS: Andrews and McMeel Publishing, 1990.

Pringle, Laurence. *The Environmental Movement: From Its Roots to the Challenges of a New Century.* New York: HarperCollins Juvenile Books, 2000.

Pringle, Laurence. *Global Warming: The Threat of Earth's Changing Climate.* New York: SeaStar Publishing Company, 2001.

Wollard, Kathy. *How Come? Planet Earth.* New York: Workman Publishing Company, 1999.

Web Sites

United States Environmental Protection Agency: Global Warming

www.epa.gov/globalwarming

This is a great place to start when looking for answers about the environment. Log on to this site to find out how global warming affects individuals and communities. Also check out links to other Web sites that deal with the greenhouse effect, pollution, and related topics.

Global Warming: Understanding the Forecast

www.edf.org/pubs/Brochures/GlobalWarming

This Web site offers a virtual museum tour of the effects of global warming. The tour provides pictures to help cyber-guests visualize exactly what is happening in the atmosphere.

RESOURCES

Organizations
Greenpeace
702 H Street, NW
Washington, DC 20001
(800) 326-0959
www.greenpeace.org
Greenpeace provides information about activities across the planet that are affecting the environment. Write to them or log onto their Web site to find out how you can help clean up the environment.

Sierra Club
85 Second Street, 2nd Floor
San Francisco, CA 94105-3441
(415) 977-5500
www.sierraclub.com

The Alliance to Save Energy
1200 18th Street, NW, Suite 900
Washington, DC 20036
(202) 857-0666

INDEX

INDEX

About The Author

Katherine Friedman was born in an environmentally conscious household in Los Angeles, CA. She currently lives in New York, NY, where she works as a freelance writer and fights pollution in her spare time.